Animal Fun Facts

FUN FACTS ABOUT BIG CATS

by Julie Murray

Dash! LEVELED READERS
An Imprint of Abdo Zoom • abdobooks.com

2

Dash!
LEVELED READERS

Level 1 – Beginning
Short and simple sentences with familiar words or patterns for children who are beginning to understand how letters and sounds go together.

Level 2 – Emerging
Longer words and sentences with more complex language patterns for readers who are practicing common words and letter sounds.

Level 3 – Transitional
More developed language and vocabulary for readers who are becoming more independent.

THIS BOOK CONTAINS RECYCLED MATERIALS

abdobooks.com

Published by Abdo Zoom, a division of ABDO, PO Box 398166, Minneapolis, Minnesota 55439.

Printed in the United States of America, North Mankato, Minnesota.
052021
092021

Photo Credits: iStock, Science Source, Shutterstock
Production Contributors: Kenny Abdo, Jennie Forsberg, Grace Hansen, John Hansen
Design Contributors: Candice Keimig, Neil Klinepier

Library of Congress Control Number: 2020919493

Publisher's Cataloging in Publication Data

Names: Murray, Julie, author.
Title: Fun facts about big cats / by Julie Murray
Description: Minneapolis, Minnesota : Abdo Zoom, 2022 | Series: Animal fun facts | Includes online resources and index.
Identifiers: ISBN 9781098224462 (lib. bdg.) | ISBN 9781098225407 (ebook) | ISBN 9781098225872 (Read-to-Me ebook)
Subjects: LCSH: Big cats--Juvenile literature. | Phantom cats--Juvenile literature. | Questions and answers--Juvenile literature. | Animal behavior--Juvenile literature.
Classification: DDC 599.75--dc23

Table of Contents

Fun Facts About Big Cats

What do jaguars, leopards, lions, and tigers have in common? They are the only big cats that roar!

Lions have the loudest roars. A lion can be heard from 5 miles (8 km) away!

The black panther is not its own **species**. It is a leopard or jaguar that is black in color.

Cheetahs are the fastest land animal. They can go from 0 to 60 miles per hour (0 to 10.2 kph) in just three seconds!

Leopards are good climbers. They spend a lot of time in trees. They often sleep in trees!

Tiger stripes are like human fingerprints. No two tigers have the same stripe pattern.

Snow leopards have five inches (12.7 cm) of **thick** fur on their bodies. This keeps them warm in the mountains of central Asia.

The clouded leopard is the smallest big cat. Males are around 3.5 feet long (1.1 m). They can weigh up to 55 pounds (25 kg).

Tigers are the largest cat **species** in the world. **Siberian tigers** are the biggest of all.

Males can be 15 feet long (4.6 m). They can weigh 660 pounds (300 kg)!

Animal Spotlight

Jaguars

Size: 4 to 7 feet (1.2-2.1 m) long; Up to 250 pounds (113.4 kg)

Appearance: tan or orange fur with dark rosette markings, powerful body, shorter legs.

Top Speed: 50 mph (80 km/h)

Range: Southwest US, Central America, South America

Habitat: rainforests, swamps, grasslands

Diet: carnivore, including mammals, fish, and reptiles.

Glossary

rosette – found on some animals' fur, a marking that is shaped like a rose.

Siberian tiger – also known as an Amur tiger, the world's largest cat that can be found in eastern Russia, China, and North Korea.

species – a group of living things that look alike, share a common name, and can have young with one another.

thick – having parts that are very close to one another.

Index

Online Resources

Booklinks
NONFICTION NETWORK
FREE! ONLINE NONFICTION RESOURCES

To learn more about big cats, please visit **abdobooklinks.com** or scan this QR code. These links are routinely monitored and updated to provide the most current information available.